Dear Parents,

Welcome to the Scholastic Reader series. We have taken over 80 years of experience with teachers, parents, and children and put it into a program that is designed to match your child's interests and skills.

Level 1—Short sentences and stories made up of words kids can sound out using their phonics skills and words that are important to remember.

Level 2—Longer sentences and stories with words kids need to know and new "big" words that they will want to know.

Level 3—From sentences to paragraphs to longer stories, these books have large "chunks" of text and are made up of a rich vocabulary.

Level 4—First chapter books with more words and fewer pictures.

It is important that children learn to read well enough to succeed in school and beyond. Here are ideas for reading this book with your child:

- Look at the book together. Encourage your child to read the title and make a prediction about the story.
- Read the book together. Encourage your child to sound out words when appropriate. When your child struggles, you can help by providing the word.
- Encourage your child to retell the story. This is a great way to check for comprehension.
- Have your child take the fluency test on the last page to check progress.

Scholastic Readers are designed to support your child's efforts to learn how to read at every age and every stage. Enjoy helping your child learn to read and love to read.

—**Francie Alexander**
Chief Education Officer
Scholastic Education

Written by Eva Moore with consultation by Joanna Cole
Illustrated by Carolyn Bracken
Designed by Peter Koblish

Based on The Magic School Bus books®
written by Joanna Cole and illustrated by Bruce Degen.

The author and editor would like to thank Kristina Timmerman of the University of Minnesota Fisheries and Wild life Department and Dave Garshelis of the Minnesota Department of Natural Resources for their expert advice in preparing this manuscript.

ISBN 978-93-5275-965-1

This edition : December 2019

Printed in India at Saurabh Printers Pvt. Ltd.

The Magic School Bus

SLEEPS FOR THE WINTER

SCHOLASTIC

It's fun to be in Ms. Frizzle's class.

Ms. Frizzle's dresses are funny.
Her shoes are funny, too.
She takes us on trips
in the Magic School Bus.

We are learning about how wild animals live in the winter. We are getting our room ready for Visitors Night.
WELCOME TO VISITORS NIGHT!
MY GRANDMA IS COMING.
ANIMALS IN WINTER
ZZZZ
MY MOM AND DAD WILL BE HERE, TOO.
BEAR DEN

"Some animals hibernate
in the winter," says Phoebe.
"Other animals stay awake,"
says Ralphie.
Ms. Frizzle gets an idea.

In no time, we are riding in the Magic School Bus. Ms. Frizzle drives north to a big park.

ANIMAL LAND PARK
DANGER
DO NOT FEED OR
DISTURB BEARS

"There's a black bear!" says Phoebe.
"There's another one," says Ralphie.

ARE BLACK BEARS BLACK?
by Dorothy Ann

Most of them are black, but some are brown, reddish, or even blond.

Then the bus starts shaking.
It makes a funny sound.
It says, "Grrrr!"

The bus has changed. Now it is the Magic School Bear!
I CAN'T BELIEVE IT!
I CAN'T *BEAR* IT!

The real bear eats some nuts.
The bus-bear eats nuts, too.

The real bear catches
a fish and eats it!
The bus-bear does, too.

The real bear eats some honey.
It even eats some bees!
Our bear does, too!

A snowflake falls.
Then more come down.
The bears find a cave.

WHY DO BEARS EAT SO MUCH?
by Arnold

Bears need to get fat in the fall.

They will live off their fat over the winter.

The bears make nests out of dry leaves.
WHY ARE WE MOVING SO SLOWLY?
YAWN

Then both bears go to sleep.
Now they are hibernating.

WHY DO ANIMALS HIBERNATE?
by Tim

Some animals — like frogs and snakes — hibernate because they would die from the cold.

Other animals — like bears — cannot find enough food in winter.

The bears sleep and sleep.
But we are not sleepy.
"Let's go outside,"
whispers the Friz.

Ms. Frizzle opens her bag.
She gives us some glasses.

They are *magic* glasses.
Now we can see
animals hibernating
under the ground!

We can see animals in logs and caves, too.

We see animals under a lake.
Then we see animals on land.
One is a big cat, a puma.
The others are wolves.

These animals are hunters.
We need help — fast!
WILD HUNTERS DON'T HURT PEOPLE . . .
. . . UNLESS THE PEOPLE GET TOO CLOSE.
I THINK WE'RE TOO CLOSE!
Salamander
Crayfish

Then we hear a growl.
It's the Magic School Bear!

We go back to the cave.
Something has happened.
IT'S AMAZING!
LOOK!
OOOH!

Two baby bears were born!
They are very small.
And they don't have fur yet.

AWAKE OR ASLEEP?
by Phoebe and Ralphie

Bears can wake up for a short time. But even then, they're still half asleep.

An animal that can wake is called a "light hibernator."

The bears are sleepy.
We are, too.
Soon we are all
fast asleep.

When we wake up, it is spring!
The bears are outside.
The baby bears play.
The mother finds food.

Ms. Frizzle drives back to school.
When we get there, it is fall again.
And the bus is a bus again.

The visitors love our room.
They love Ms. Frizzle's dress, too!

ANIMALS THAT ARE ACTIVE IN WINTER
Fox
Hare
Deer
Cardinal
Squirrel
WELCOME TO VISITORS NIGHT!
DOES MS. FRIZZLE *BUG* YOU?
NO, BUT HER DRESS DOES!

Fluency Fun

The words in each list below end in the same sounds.
Read the words in a list.
Read them again.
Read them faster.
Try to read all 15 words in one minute.

found	**driving**	**another**
round	**getting**	**beaver**
sound	**growling**	**hunter**
ground	**skating**	**mother**
around	**sleeping**	**winter**

Look for these words in the story.

animals **breathe** **people**

enough **hibernate**

Note to Parents:
According to *A Dictionary of Reading and Related Terms,* fluency is "the ability to read smoothly, easily, and readily with freedom from word-recognition problems." Fluency is necessary for good comprehension and enjoyable reading. The activities on this page include a speed drill and a sight-recognition drill. Speed drills build fluency because they help students rapidly recognize common syllables and spelling patterns in words, and they're fun! Sight-recognition drills help students smoothly and accurately recognize words. Practice these activities with your child to help him or her become a fluent reader.

–Wiley Blevins,
Reading Specialist